Loving Sex

Straight Talk for Straight Girls From Wise Women

By

Caitlin Claire Diehl

Waln Creek Publications
Salem, Oregon

ISBN-13: 978-0692218372
ISBN-10: 0692218378

Cover Art: Steven Novak

www.facebook.com/CaitlinClaireDiehl

Manufactured in the United States of America

CONTENTS

INTRODUCTION

☙

This is a sexual relationships book, not a sex manual. There will be no diagrams or tips about technique. What you will find are thoughts, reflections, stories and decidedly personal opinions about what makes for a good sexual relationship.

The intended readers of this book are young women embarking down this road for the first time, though anyone is welcome to turn the pages.

In each chapter are vignettes from various women, ranging in age from their 20's to their 70's, who were kind enough to share their coming-of-age stories in the hope that their life experience might be of use to young women starting their own journey. The words are their own, though lightly edited for spelling and grammar, and some of the names and details have been changed to respect their privacy.

The "Fact Boxes" are all snippets of information taken directly from the Kinsey Institute's website (www.kinseyinstitute.org). The Kinsey Institute, based out of Indiana University, is a well-respected research facility working towards advancing sexual health and knowledge worldwide.

When reading the book, feel free to skip around to the sections and topics that are of most use to you. My goal is for this book to be your friendly confidante—an older sister or an aunt, perhaps—who loves and supports you, wanting only the best for you as you set out to become the fabulous woman you are meant to be.

All of us women sharing stories in this book want to hold up the truth of our lives like lamps, in order to shine our light to illuminate your own, unique path.

Caitlin Claire Diehl
May 2014

FOREWORD

⋐

Dear Daughter,

I'm giving you these words and this book because I love you and want you to find all the joy there can be in sexual relationships. I also want you to avoid the mistakes I've made. Of course you will. Instead, you will make your own mistakes and find your own joys. But as I'm a woman of 50+ years, married to a man for 28 years, and the mother of a young woman about to embark on her own life away from home, I wanted to be able to sit down for a heart-to-heart and tell you all the things I've learned over the years about relationships and sex.

Like that's going to happen.

If I did, you would die of embarrassment. I'm not sure if you'll think this book is any less embarrassing. But I had to try.

I've already taught you where babies come from, what your girl parts look like and the changes that come with puberty. We've gone over sexual preference, rape, birth control, STD's, the morning after pill, and abortion. Your school has also chimed in, minus the really useful information. But these facts are just background, "book learning", if you will. They don't convey what it's really like to have sex, make love, or hook up with another person. The facts can't convey the real world experience —with all the textures, smells, hair, emotions, and bodily fluids— of getting naked and sexual with another person.

So that's what this book is for. To tell you the truth about sexual relationships, with the hope that whenever you choose to embark on this particular adventure—and whether it be with a man or another woman—that having a detailed map will help your journey be safe yet full of delightful discovery.

Love,
Mom

Chapter One

Becoming Sexually Active

❧

How Do You Know When You're Ready For Sex ?

I'm assuming that you have a choice. That you're trying to decide if and when you're ready to share your body for the first time with another person. That you're not one of many young women who have already been molested, raped, or violated in any way against your will. If that choice was taken away from you, I'm sorry. I've been there. Chapter Five talks about the extra emotions that go along with starting a sexual relationship after molestation, abuse and rape. Still, you can read this first section, too.

Maybe you're feeling frisky. You're curious. You've been making out and thinking about taking that next step or you feel like everybody but you is getting some and you want some, too. How do you know if you're ready?

A Streetcar Named Desire

First of all, our bodies are able to respond physically to sexual activity the second we go through puberty. Although we're still growing and developing for several years, the hormones that stand up and dance when we're sexually attracted to somebody are good to go as soon as we've crossed the puberty starting line.

> At any given point in time, most U.S. adolescents are not engaging in partnered sexual behavior. While 40% of 17 year-old males reported vaginal intercourse in the past year, only 27% reported the same in the past 90 days. By their late teenage years, at least 3/4 of all men and women have had intercourse, and more than 2/3 of all sexually experienced teens have had 2 or more partners.

In fact, desire is usually the easy part. The sex drive is a powerful automobile that just cruises faster and faster along naked highway. It can feel GREAT letting those engines rev to full throttle, letting yourself be a passenger in the car when your sexual feelings are behind the wheel. For some people.

For others, those feelings of desire can be scary, overwhelming and hard to make sense of. Sexual feelings can feel like a loss of control or, depending on how you were raised, can leave you feeling ashamed or uncomfortable.

So, the first and easiest thing to assess is your own level of desire and how comfortable you are experiencing your sexual feelings.

Julie Says:
The first time a boy kissed me I felt fully alive for the first time. I was awake and present in my whole body in a way I never experienced before. I LOVED making out!

That Which Cannot Be Named

I'm referring, of course, to masturbation, also known as self-gratification or self-pleasuring. Some religions proscribe against it. If your religion doesn't, and you have no other objections, by all means, take care of business yourself. It's fast, efficient, cheap and easy (so you don't have to be!). Pleasuring yourself is a good way to learn about your own sexual response before you ever have a partner, or a way to take the edge off during a dry spell. Even when having regular sex with a partner (or partners), many people still masturbate.

> *Parker Lee Says:*
> *My sex talk consisted of my mother giving a me a large picture book with drawn characters and pretty much all I remember learning was masturbation is BAD! NOT good. NOT necessary. A big fat NO-NO. So okay, I hear ya. I had not done anything like that yet so okay, one more thing for a good Christian girl to steer clear of. So noted.*

In a study of undergraduate college students, 98% of men and 44% of women reported having ever masturbated. Among undergraduate students, men reported masturbating an average of 12 times per month, while women reported an average of 4.7 times per month.

More than half of women ages 18 to 49 reported masturbating during the previous 90 days. Rates were highest among those 25-29 and progressively lesser in older age groups.

13

Will She or Won't She?

Desire is the starting point in deciding whether or not you're ready to take another step towards being sexually intimate. As you answer the following questions, you'll get a better sense of your own comfort with sexual feelings.

Questions:
- Do you experience sexual desire?
- How comfortable are you with those feelings?
- Are you comfortable with self-gratification and know how to please yourself?
- Is there someone in your life who stirs those feelings in you?
- Is this person attracted to you?

However, there is so much more to a sexual connection with another person than physical desire.

I Heart You

Baring one's body usually involves baring one's emotions, especially for young women. For young men, not so much. The stereotype is that men use love to get sex and women use sex to get love. Getting naked with someone becomes emotionally intimate when both parties also bare their feelings, when there's affection as well as attraction. Not everybody needs or wants to unbutton their clothes and their emotions at the same time so what's important is to know what you need and what your expectations are, as well as those of your intended partner.

With years of sexual experience, a history of past sexual abuse, or any other emotional scars, people learn to separate their bodily sensations from emotional feelings in order to have sex without caring so much, or at least pretending not to care, but that is a sad road to travel.

How much better to embark on a journey of sexual discovery with someone you care about and who cares about you.

Of course, this assumes some introspection on your part, some looking before you leap, and a degree of relationship before you even jump into bed. However, that's not how everybody operates. Some of us think less and discover our own preferences through trial and error, through morning-after regrets and delightful discoveries. Here are some questions to help you clarify what you want in a relationship.

Questions:

- ◆ Do you like the person you want to have sex with?
- ◆ Is the feeling mutual?
- ◆ Do you want to entrust your heart and your body to this person?
- ◆ Are you hoping for a relationship or is just hooking up okay?
- ◆ Is the feeling mutual?
- ◆ Do you enjoy what physical intimacy you've had so far?
- ◆ Can you imagine feeling comfortable being naked with this person?

Flowers, Candlelight and Bodily Fluids

So you feel desire, you have a prospect in mind, but is it sex you really want? There is quite a difference between romance and sex, though the two can co-exist quite happily.

15

Romance movies show the hearts and flowers aspect of relationships, the emotional expression of love and tenderness. If there's naked sex, it's beautiful and gentle or steamy and passionate. That's what makes many young women melt and what many hope for when embarking on their first sexual relationship.

When many young women imagine a sexual relationship, what they're really longing for is love and romance, the feeling of being cherished and desired. In romance movies, if the guy brings flowers, it means he really cares. In real life, romantic gestures may or may not indicate genuine feeling. Even when a guy really cares, the language of romance doesn't necessarily translate well into the language of sex. The language of romance and the language of sex are two different dialects. The sweaty and grunty reality of sexual activity—even when there is genuine affection—doesn't always match candlelight fantasies.

For example, I'm here to tell you that bodily fluids—sweat, semen and vaginal secretions—all have an odor and that odor is different for each person. Sexual chemistry usually means you won't be repulsed by, and likely will enjoy, the scent of your sex partner. But since movies don't usually do Smell-a-Vision, you should be prepared for that dimension. People also pass gas during sex. Sad but true. That also smells.

Furthermore, those smells are wafting from private parts that look funny and have unfortunate names, either too clinical or appallingly crude. However, if you can't say "penis," you shouldn't be messing around with one, and that goes for your "vagina", too!

Hair is also a factor. Long hair gets tangled up in zippers and clothing and trapped in kissing mouths. Close contact with pubic hair also leaves stray hairs in your mouth. Scruffy faces are quite prickly, beards can be soft or coarse, and mustaches can poke into your nose. Unwaxed men have varying amounts of hair on their chests and abdomens and some also grow it on their backs and backsides. Women, too! Is it a turn on or a turn off? You decide.

Being comfortable with noise is also a must for engaging in sex and I don't mean talking, though that would be great, too. Right now in the United States, if a movie couple is going to have sex and the movie is to receive a PG-13 rating, no sex noises are allowed. That is a far cry from real life (pun intended)! Noises you might make or hear during sex include moans, gasps, sighs, crying out with pleasure, crying tears because moved (or frustratingly disappointed), laughter—with each other rather than at each other, I hope—the occasional "Ouch!", as well as words of encouragement or direction (harder, faster, slower, softer, over here, not there, what in God's name are you doing?).

Sexual activity is embodied activity. While there is also a mental and emotional component to sex, in order to be sure you can deal with the body part (ha ha), I recommend asking yourself some earthy questions:

Questions:
- Do I know how my body smells when it's clean and when it's not?
- Do I like how my partner smells?
- How do I feel about bodily functions?
- Am I saying yes to sex when what I really want is romance?

My Place, Yours or the Back Seat of My Best Friend's Car

Logistics are also something rarely dealt with in romance movies. Erica Jong is a writer who made famous the term "zipless f**k" to describe the phenomenon of clothes magically melting away when two movie or book characters are getting busy. The reality is always much more complicated. Bra hooks won't unhook and then get stuck in somebody's sweater. Skinny jeans can't easily be pulled off by either party, especially if you've forgotten to take off your shoes. For some reason, socks are always the last bit of clothing to be discarded, which some find hilarious rather than arousing.

Also, where is this disrobing taking place? In a car? Your parents' house when they're gone? Behind a tree in the park? Your dorm room? Does somebody—please please please—have their own place?

What about how much time you can devote to this encounter? In the movies, most sexual encounters are two minutes long and result in both partners achieving satisfaction. Talk about a fantasy! So, are you wanting a quickie or a marathon session? Do you have time for what you need or will you feel rushed? (Feeling rushed and getting stressed out vs. being in a rush because you can't wait are two different experiences).

Furthermore, how much privacy do you have? Do doors lock, windows have curtains, walls have soundproofing? Are others going to be aware of what you're up to and do you care? Though "discovery fantasies" are quite common, decide how much of an exhibitionist you are and insist on the privacy, timetable and discretion you need.

Linda Says:
One day, while in the midst of my high school years and
dating the same boy for over a year, my mom and I were
talking about sex. She reminded me that if we thought
we would be able to use my bedroom, that wasn't going
to happen. She wondered aloud how it would be to have
sex in the '65 Mustang. She also reminded me that once
we went all the way, there was no going backward. Once
you take it to full sex, you aren't going to just want to
make out.

Like a Virgin

For some reason, popular culture holds heterosexual intercourse to be the definition of sex. Former President Clinton's infamous line, "I did not have sex with that woman," proclaimed that no sexual intercourse had been on the menu, though the other items

Considerations of "sex" also varied depending on whether or not a condom was used, female or male orgasm, and if the respondent was performing or receiving the stimulation.

With participants ranging from 18 to 96 years, the oldest and youngest groups of men were less likely to consider some behaviors as "sex".

with that White House intern were varied and plentiful. To someone of this mindset, "having sex" equals "having intercourse". In our culture, young men and women who have not participated in heterosexual intercourse count themselves virgins, no matter how extensive and acrobatic their other sexual escapades.

"Technical virginity" often means "everything, but…", allowing the "virgin" to feel virtuous (and perhaps live up

19

to familial and/or religious/moral convictions) while still getting his or her sexual needs met (or meeting those of a partner). I don't get it, but I accept that women and men often keep those kinds of mental records.

However, I am here to tell you that if you are doing ANYTHING of a sexual nature with another person, you're sexually active, whether or not you've had intercourse. I, personally, don't want you to be splitting hairs (not with the hairs again!). If you want to be sexual, then go ahead. Don't wear a grammatical chastity belt.

> There is wide variability in what people consider included in "having sex". In a recent study at The Kinsey Institute, nearly 45% of participants considered performing manual-genital stimulation to be "having sex," 71% considered performing oral sex to be "sex," 80.8% for anal-genital intercourse.

Abstinence by Choice

Within American pop culture, being sexual is expected, celebrated, flaunted and exploited to sell just about everything. Pop culture is loud, colorful and ubiquitous. Consequently, choosing not to partake in sexual activity (abstinence) can feel like a solitary road because it seems like "everybody is doing it". Unless you're wearing a "promise ring" or belong to a "virginity club", no one else knows the other travelers on the abstinence road.

The truth is, not everybody is doing it. Many people have solid moral and religious reasons why they prefer abstinence. Perhaps they are waiting until they marry or have chosen abstinence as a way of life. Other young men and

Percent of population having had first intercourse by age:

MALES	FEMALES
25% by age 15	26% by age 15
37% by age 16	40% by age 16
46% by age 17	49% by age 17
62% by age 18	70% by age 18
69% by age 19	77% by age 19
85% by age 20-21	81% by age 20-21
89% by age 22-24	92% by age 22-24

women want to wait until they're in a committed relationship with someone they love and respect, who loves and respects them in return. Sometimes a history of child sexual abuse and/or rape can result in a lack of interest in being sexually active as an adult. Some people have a low libido or none at all and just don't care enough to get sexual. Sorting out one's sexual preference can be confusing for some and result in less sexual activity.

The best thing about choosing abstinence is that it *is* a choice, not a permanent condition. Until you find the right person, until the time is right, until you feel ready, it is more than okay to focus on other aspects of your life. This is true whether you're considering embarking on your first sexual relationship or you're taking a time out in-between partners.

Sarah Says:
Finding a man is not on my priority list. I believe joining

my life to another ought to be a blessing for both of us, a gift on top of an already fulfilling existence full of fun, interesting projects, and love, not to complete it. If I meet someone along that road and we love each other, then I will have another great joy in my life. Living a life of abstinence has its own gifts, things I've come to value. I have so much fun pursuing my passions, working on projects, and traveling without taking anyone else into account. With all that time and energy normally spent on a relationship, I can invest instead in the world and the people around me—giving my love out and going on adventures. My unfulfilled need for physical closeness and intimacy has also drawn me into God's arms innumerable times. Being more aware of God's presence and feeling his/her closeness has given me abiding strength, deep comfort, and lasting joy for this is true intimacy and our time together has become my center, my ballast, my life.

Abstinence by Default

The other thing I'll blame on American pop culture is that being seen as sexually desirable is portrayed as the highest good. The ultimate compliment is, "You're hot!" *People* magazine devotes a whole issue to the "Sexiest Man Alive", not the "Smartest" or the "Kindest" or the "Best To Call When Your Car Breaks Down." Currently in pop culture, physical attractiveness and charisma rate far higher than strength of character or nobility of purpose.

This is a problem because it implies that only by being attractive to others are we worthy, that our lives will only have meaning if others (preferably lots of others) think we're sexy. This is just not true. Sex is just one aspect of life and it is only more or less important according to individual preferences and life stages. As I'm sure you've heard before, there's more to life than sex.

The truth is that while sexuality is a part of being human, not everybody will be able to express that in a relationship. Not everyone has a partner or will ever have a partner. Not everyone finds that special someone or anyone at all.

This might be sad. This might be just fine, but I think it's important to mention it just in case you don't ever have the opportunity to connect sexually with someone.

Rachel Says:
I was never with somebody I wanted to marry. I was in two very long-term relationships where the other person wanted us to get married and, well, I loved both people very much and I loved our relationship. I was really clear I didn't want to be married to them, and marry my life to their life.

Somehow I had this clarity that was at the soul level or something like that, that my spirit knows that I was going to be happier honoring and keeping the strength of my own spirit. That is going to make me be at peace in life. And happy. Rather than finding my happiness through pairing up with somebody else.

Feeling Empowered vs. Feeling Pressured

I hope you're thinking about starting a sexual relationship because there's somebody that makes both your heart and hormones go pitter pat and the feeling is mutual. If you want a real relationship rather than just a hook-up, let yourself progress slowly through the stages of physical contact while you figure out what the relationship means, if anything. Holding hands, hugging, kissing, being arm-in-arm (and talking!) are important ways of letting yourself grow in closeness before any clothing comes off.

Often, however, only one of those—heart or hormones—is sufficient to begin peeling off garments. The key is to be aware of your own feelings, desires and needs as well as those of your *amour*. When you're acting out of a place of free choice—and so is your partner—the positive energy you feel is unmistakable, even if you might be nervous or scared. Taking the step to be sexually active for the first time, or with a brand new partner, is very empowering when done by choice for the right reasons.

Unfortunately, many young women have early experiences of being pressured for sex. To be fair, I imagine the same thing is true for some young men as well. Pressure feels like a weight, cornering you, closing off your options. The pressure might be emotional found in phrases such as: "You would if you loved me;" "I have needs;" "If you won't meet my needs, so-and-so will;" and "Everybody's doing it." Pressure might be physical with sexual activity continuing after one party says no or by being held down.

Once pressure turns physical or emotional pressure turns into coercion with implied or explicit threats against

More than half the participants in the 2010 national sex survey ages 18-24 indicated that their most recent sexual partner was a casual or dating partner.

For all other age groups, the majority of study participants indicated that their most recent sexual partner was a relationship partner.

your safety or that of others, then the behavior becomes sexual assault. I'll talk more about that in Chapter 5.

If getting busy with someone feels positive, uplifting, fun—and not just in the moment but afterwards as well—then you know you're making an empowered choice that's right for you.

> *MaryKate Says:*
> *As far as sex goes—I know what the modern approach is—make sure it's someone that you love and then everything will be fine. I totally disagree. As far as what my friends have told me—they wish they hadn't. The guys change while the girls become super attached and their judgment of the merit of their man gets cloudy. Then it gets too complicated afterwards. Even my little sister's "sophisticated" New York friends say the same thing. So my advice is not to have sex if they are young women in college—once they're in their 20's maybe they can handle it emotionally and it will be no big deal. They should focus on their schoolwork while they're in college so they can be the best versions of themselves.*

Be Prepared

Part of being an empowered, choice-making woman is to be not only emotionally prepared for sexual activity but practically as well. I'm talking about birth control and Sexually Transmitted Diseases/Infections (STD/STI) protection. Condoms are your friend. Carry them in your purse or backpack. Stash them in your bedside table. That way, you'll have them available if and when you decide to get busy, and you won't be tempted to have unprotected sex. If you are confident enough to go into a store and look the checkout clerk in the eye as you buy condoms, then you are well on your way to being adult enough to handle sexual activity.

The Center for Disease Control and Prevention estimates that 19 million new sexually-transmitted infections occur each year, almost half of them among young people ages 15-24.
By the age of 24, one in three sexually active people will have contracted an STI.

Chapter Two

Sexual Preference

☙

Choosing a Team

Figuring out your sexual preference can run the gamut from easy-peasy to downright confusing. Before we get into a discussion of why, let's make sure we're clear on terms, first.

- *Homosexual* people prefer to have sexual relationships with people of the same sex, men with men, women with women.
- *Heterosexuals* prefer someone of the opposite sex (men with women).
- *Bisexuals* are sexually attracted to both men and women.

Scientists tell us that sexual preference is a continuum with people arranged all along this line, from decidedly heterosexual or homosexual on each end and varying degrees of bisexuality as one approaches the middle. Cultural attitudes, family and religious values, as well as changing circumstances can all influence just where someone places herself or himself on that continuum.

In an analysis of national survey results from 2006-2008, the percentage reporting their sexual identity as homosexual ranged from 2% to 4% of males, and about 1% to 2% of females.

The percentage reporting their sexual identity as bisexual is between 1% and 3% of males, and 2% to 5% of females.

While scientists tell us that sexual *preference* is biologically based, sexual *behavior* is multiply determined. In other words, choices about who to get sexual with are often based on far more than simple biology. Affection, attraction, opportunity, drugs, alcohol, loneliness, sorrow, exuberance, curiosity, anger: These and more can influence sexual choices, including your choice of a sexual partner.

Women as Friends, Women as Lovers

Many women I know prefer the company of women to men, even those women married to men they love. There can be a sisterhood among women that is uniquely fulfilling and quite different from what can be experienced in relationships with men. Not always, of course. Some men are quite nurturing. Women can also be competitive and backstabbing. But I'm talking about positive relationships between women. Usually young women have more female friends than male friends. When one's sexuality is unfolding, this can be confusing sometimes. Preferring the company of women doesn't necessarily mean you're a lesbian.

Nancy Says:
How did I know I was or wasn't gay? I didn't even think of this until after college—way after, like when

I was 30. But then at that time, I realized much to my surprise, that I had feelings that weren't just "meeting a new friend" feeling for a woman with whom I worked, who was gay and kept putting her hand on my thigh when we drove around. She always talked about a woman she was interested in, so I was confused and didn't know how to interpret her flirtation. But I knew I LIKED the flirting. Then I asked a woman out. Then a woman asked me out. Then I went out with a guy. Then I met another guy and we fell in love. We're married now. I didn't think anything of my desire/curiosity in other women; I just knew that I was attracted to good people and didn't need to have a label that said I was gay or straight or bi; I just liked good people and liked my now-husband more than anyone else. I don't know if it's that important to 'know' if you're gay. Just know that you're open to feeling love energy from anyone and accept what comes your way.

Some Things to Think About

If you're wondering if you're straight, gay or bi, ask yourself these questions:

- ♦ When I'm fantasizing about having sex, who do I fantasize about?
- ♦ If I've had crushes on movie stars or book characters, which sex were they?
- ♦ Who in my real life makes my girl parts stand up and take notice?
- ♦ Do I like kissing (or the idea of kissing) guys? How about girls?

♦   Which is more of a turn-on: Getting up close
     and personal with a penis or a vagina? Or none-
     of-the-above?

Figuring out your sexual identity can be a process that takes time and experience. Let yourself take all the time you need to figure out who you are as a sexual being.

CHAPTER THREE

DATING AND SEX

☯

Is "Casual Sex" Ever Casual?

Having casual sex means no commitment to a relationship and sometimes no actual feelings for the other person beyond physical attraction. I hear that some people are just fine with this. I am not so sure. My observation is that this kind of situation is actually far more emotionally complicated than it seems.

Friends With Benefits: When two people have regular sex but no "relationship", more often than not, one person is more emotionally invested than the other but is settling for what he or she can get. Eventually this person will feel used. Cue drama and heartbreak. Not always, though.

Nancy Says:
I 'dated around' in high school. I had a few boyfriends who took me to movies and the high school dances. I was monogamous, but I could turn on a dime if I got cold feet or lost interest or... One time I spent a band bus ride making out with a trumpet player and told him I'd see him at the dance that night. But I didn't go——he

was sort of nerdy – and really never spoke to him again. Dating around went on through college. I was never serious with anyone, never felt like my heart belonged with anyone, never wanted to be held to a commitment and lose the independent years of living/experiencing ahead of me.

And I was a feminist by golly. My Body Myself, *free love, make love not war were embraced. And I LOVED to kiss and eventually, after my freshman year in college, I LOVED to have sex. I loved the heavy weight of a man lying on top of me; I loved being kissed on the neck and ears. I could go on…. it was playful, recreational sex. But I want to be very clear that I was monogamous with these various college (and beyond) lovers. That was hugely important to me; it represented some sort of idea that I wasn't just sleeping around. Plus, there was a connection with the various guys, a respect and a loyalty about sharing the incredible and intimate experience that I couldn't trivialize by going back and forth between guys.*

One Night Stands: This is not usually a recipe for a great sexual experience, especially if it's one or both person's first sexual experience. However, there are always exceptions to "usually". Sometimes people are less inhibited if they know they won't ever see their partner again. Some people, usually extroverts, just relish connecting with others, even if only sexually.

Alexa Says:
When I was in college, I went on a study abroad program. On the flight I met a girl who came out to me

as a lesbian and we became good friends and hung out a lot. One day I got to talking with her telling her that I hadn't had sex forever and she said I should have sex for my birthday, which was coming up. I was like, "I'm not going to have sex with some random guy." She said, "What about somebody in our program? Do you like anyone?" I responded, "Yeah, I kind of do," and I told her who. Well, unbeknownst to me, she approached that guy and basically pimped me out to him.

In my dorm room that night, I heard a knock on the window and it was that guy! He said, "Hey, you want to hang out?" I thought for a minute, told myself what the heck, and snuck out. We went to the library, one of the few buildings open late, and had a tryst in the stacks. It was totally on the down low. Nobody knew about it except us, which made it a fun little secret. He was my birthday present to myself and he knew it and he was game. We didn't do it again, never talked about it, and just smiled knowingly at each other now and again.

For certain phases of my life when I wasn't in an exclusive relationship with anybody, I definitely enjoyed the fruits of the world. After my study abroad program I can remember telling my mom, with great joy and wonder, that there was just a whole world of men out there. My mom smiled at me and said, "Halleluiah!"

Sex for Sex's Sake

Women get horny, just like men do. Sometimes you might just want to get laid and there is nothing wrong with those feelings. Whether you have a moral objection to acting on those feelings, I leave up to you. I do think that casual sex can be an emotional mine field, and it is in this area that

women really need to be very self-aware as to their emotional expectations.

In my decidedly married, old-fashioned opinion, sex
might start as casual in the minds of those involved, but it
never ends up that way. While it is possible to divorce your
emotions from the physical act of sex, and guys tend to be
much better at that than women, why would you want to?
Using another person as simply an outlet for physical sexual
tensions cheapens them and you. To my mind, sex is usually
best when it is a physical expression of emotional connection, especially the first time. But not always. So, as always,
know yourself and what level of emotional connection and
intimacy you need from sexual activity.

Alexa Says:
*If you're going to have casual sex, you really have to have
the right attitude. Don't let yourself get attached. Go
into it knowing what it is and what it isn't. Protect your
heart. Keep yourself open to the experience but detach
from any expectation of it turning into a relationship.
Know what you're signing up for. Most importantly, be
safe. Don't put yourself in a vulnerable position. I have
to say that while I never consciously went out to get lucky,
when the opportunity arose, I jumped on it. So to speak.*

MaryKate Says:
*My boyfriend had been one of my best friends in college
and had a girlfriend then—meanwhile he spent all his
time with me. It was total BS. At the end of college, he
broke up with his girlfriend to date me, then said he was
just a player but he still loved me blah blah blah... etc.
etc. It was lame all round. So—stay away from guys*

with girlfriends! But if you find someone with whom you can be yourself—keep him around!

Is it Love or Lust?

This is THE question I'd wished someone had talked over with me growing up. I didn't realize, naïve Catholic girl that I was, that it was possible to lust after someone without loving them. I assumed if I lusted, I loved, and vice versa. Soooo not true. And maybe you know that already.

Yes, it's possible to be a straight woman, love a guy and not want to have sex with him. He's like a brother to you, like family, a best friend. In the movies, this guy either ends up being "the one" or he falls for your best friend. This is a common plot because while men and women can be "just friends" it's often more than that for one of the pair. Sometimes when young men and women pal around, there is sexual attraction but no one is acting on it or it's one-sided. Just make sure you know your heart and aren't trampling on his.

Lust, I'm happy to say, can be experienced at any time for the most unexpected people, even when you're in a committed relationship with someone else. Lust is chemical and a delightful sensation. Following through on that lust is a choice, not an imperative. You don't have to act on lustful feelings. Lust is just one factor to consider when making sexual choices.

Julie Says:
I was participating in a team-building exercise with some fellow college students that involved pairing up with each person in the group, closing our eyes, and feeling each others' hands and forearms. I don't remember now what the point was but what I do remember is the incredible

sexual charge I shared with one fellow. The chemistry was palpable, as if our hands and arms were electrified. But when I opened my eyes and saw who it was, my instant reaction was, "Ewww". Not because I didn't like how he looked, but because I didn't like him as a person. At all. I was very disturbed that I could have such a physical rush from someone I didn't even like. He, of course, wanted very much to repeat that electrifying experience and I had to dodge him for weeks.

Sisters Before Misters

"Sisters before misters" is a statement of sexual ethics. It means you don't sleep with another girl's guy. It means you don't dump plans with a girlfriend to hang with your guy instead. It means you keep your friends' confidences and not repeat them to your man. Basically, don't put your friendships (or the rest of your life) on hold simply because you have a boyfriend.

Balancing a new love relationship alongside old friendships and work, school or family responsibilities can be a juggling act. New love is all-consuming and there is only so much time in a day after all. However, when you're young, men often come and go while girlfriends stick. So be a loyal and trustworthy friend. Besides, if you drop your girlfriends, who's going to go shoe shopping or do shots with you when you and your guy break up?

Alexa Says:
This story makes me sound sluttish but here it is. There I was, freshman year of college, and had just started dating a bunch of different guys. I'd been dating one

of those guys for maybe a few weeks when I was eating lunch in the cafeteria and a cute, bouncy girl came over to see me. She said, "Can I talk to you? It's kind of private." I said sure and we went outside. She said, "I know you're dating this guy. I was, too, and I wanted to let you know that I've just been diagnosed with gonorrhea and I've been letting people know." I thought that was really cool of her. I didn't get gonorrhea and that guy and I didn't last, but Laura became one of my best friends all through college and beyond. So that's my story of The Gonorrhea Scare of 1984.

Playing the Field

I only ever had boyfriends I was serious about and I married my college sweetheart so I don't have much experience concurrently dating more than one man. I've heard it can be quite fun.

Alexa Says:
My freshman year was the Year of the Three Steves. I was dating three different guys at the same time, all named Steve. None of them knew about the others; none of it was serious. The only hard part of juggling three guys was knowing which one was calling me, back in the days before cell phones and Caller ID. The phone would ring and the guy would say, "This is Steve," and I couldn't really ask, "Which one?" I'd have to play it really cool, say things like, "Where are you calling from?" since they lived in different parts of town, or "What are you doing?" because that would give me a clue which one it was. It was all pretty funny.

MaryKate Says:
Go on as many dates as possible with different guys.
These days girls and guys are serial monogamists. There
is no such thing as dating around which is such a shame
because then some miss out on what might really work!

Practice Makes Perfect

Being a skilled lover takes practice, patience, perseverance, and a sense of humor. Whether that practice is with one partner or many, nobody is born knowing how to pleasure another person or what will please you. Inexperienced guys' usual technique consists of trying to swallow your tonsils accompanied by breast and butt grabbing, topped off with a laser-like determination to insert part A into part B as quickly as possible. That's the linear road their sex drive prefers. Biologically speaking, men's arousal patterns are fairly straightforward and easily activated, whereas the arousal patterns of women tend to be more idiosyncratic and easily derailed.

About 85% of men report that their partner had an orgasm at the most recent sexual event. This compares to the 64% of women who report having had an orgasm at their most recent sexual event. (A difference that is too large to be accounted for by some of the men having had male partners at their most recent event.) Men are more likely to orgasm when sex includes vaginal intercourse; women are more likely to orgasm when they engage in a variety of sex acts and when oral sex or vaginal intercourse is included.

> Many women express that their most satisfying sexual experiences entail being connected to someone, rather than solely basing satisfaction on orgasm.

If the way your sex partner touches you isn't doing it for you, you have to decide if the problem is that the guy just doesn't turn you on or if it's his technique that leaves you contemplating the homework you haven't yet finished. If it's the guy you can't stand, do yourselves a favor and make your excuses and leave. If it's his technique, then you're going to have get over your embarrassment, break the cone of silence and give him a little direction.

In turn, ask for some guidance for yourself. The plumbing on men and women is different, and individual men and women are turned on by different types of touch. Part of what makes for good sex is a mutual sensitivity to each other's needs and wants. Whether you're with a guy for one night or many nights, taking the time to communicate your needs and to ask about his will make for a much more enjoyable connection.

Parker Lee Says:
At 19 I got married to my first real boyfriend. I didn't know how to ask for what I needed or wanted. Even if I knew how to ask, I didn't know what to ask for. I was unsure and uneducated. I only knew what he had taught me, which, looking back, wasn't a whole lot (bless his 20-year-old heart). I was not satisfied in our sex life; I had romanticized so much more than what we had. Neither was he [satisfied with our sex life], as evidenced by the string of girlfriends he had during our marriage.

Falling for the First Time

I can't promise you that the first time you have intercourse it'll be great sex. If your hymen is still intact, then it can be temporarily painful the first time penis meets vagina. Plus, the first time people try anything there's always a fair amount of trial and error. Having ecstatic, orgasmic sex the first time you fall into bed is mostly the stuff of fiction. That's why I think the personal connection with the guy is the most important factor when you decide you're ready to have intercourse for the first time. If you care about each other, then the feeling of closeness and connection that sex engenders, whether or not you orgasm, can be really lovely and enough to tide you over until you've spent more time in bed and learned your way around each other's bodies.

Chapter Four

Dating Pitfalls

℃

Hopping the Train to Slutsville

Whether or not you're labeled a slut, or a guy is judged as a man-whore, is a result of the meeting point between sexual behavior and other people's value judgments. Women often have it especially tough because being comfortable with one's sexuality and expressing that can be perceived as acting slutty. One person's "adventurous" is someone else's "slutty". Finding ways to express your sexuality without drawing negative judgment from others can be a tough line to walk and you'll need to find your own balance.

While I'm not a big fan of listening to the haters, I do think the social norms that underlie these negative labels are a clue to what constitutes ethical sexual behavior. While it's important to experience life, it's more important to be someone who treats yourself and others with respect. Being "easy" or indiscriminate in sexual partners communicates to others that you lack self-respect.

Here are the behaviors that, when noticed by others, tend to put you on that S-Train:

- Having sex with anyone who asks
- Having sex with a different guy every night, or every week, or (possibly) every month
- Having sex with multiple guys simultaneously (group sex)
- Cheating on your boyfriend
- Cheating with another woman's boyfriend
- Getting drunk or high regularly and then having sex
- Getting an STD/STI
- Getting pregnant intentionally to "trap" a guy
- Waking up next to a guy who's name you don't know
- Waking up in bed with a guy not knowing how you got there

I'm sure many people have done at least one of these at one time or another during their growing up years. We all make choices when we're young that as we mature, we might look back on and regret. What crowns you a slut is a pattern of such behavior—repeated acts of using people and discarding them like Kleenex, without regard to the emotional or physical consequences for yourself or your partners.

Alice Says:
I share with my daughters that every relationship they enter into will become an indelible part of their life "history." There is no way to erase the memory of a relationship (good or bad) and the "emotional baggage" that every individual carries with her throughout life which is a compilation of the experiences and those relationships.

- Males 30-44 report an average of 6-8 female sexual partners in their lifetime.
- Females 30-44 report an average of 4 male sexual partners
  in their lifetime.

Pooping in the Pool

Don't date or have sex with your boss, a prospective em-
ployer, your professor, graduate students if you're an un-
dergrad, your thesis advisor, or anyone who has any power
over your life, especially if he is married but even if he is
not. No matter how smart it might seem at the time, or how
compelling the attraction, it's not worth it. Ever.

Not only do sexual harassment laws and professional
standards prohibit this behavior, the more important point
is that it is going to backfire and become a disaster of epic
proportions that you will forever regret. Don't do it.

If there is mutual attraction between you and whoever
this powerful person is, wait to get involved until after you
are clear of their influence on your future. Then you will
clearly see how real the attraction is.

The Morning After

One way to tell if the sex you had was a mistake is how you
feel about it the next day. Are you crawling out of bed—
his or yours—feeling deliciously sated and happy? Are you
blushing with delight as you recall your sexcapades? Are you
filled with terrible regret, sneaking around trying to avoid
the "walk of shame" as you head home in the morning in
the clothes you wore the night before, not wanting anyone
to see you? Worst of all, are you panicking because you had

unprotected sex and are terrified you're going to get pregnant or an STD?

Unprotected sex is always a huge mistake because no
matter how lovely it is in the moment, the reckoning always
comes in the form of massive stress as you rush out to buy
the morning-after pill, or if you're opposed to that, anxious-
ly wait for your period to arrive, which is certain to be late
because you're so stressed, not to mention having to pop into
the health center to get tested for HIV, Chlamydia, gonorrhea, herpes, and all the rest.

A study at The Kinsey Institute found some of the most common
problems with condom use to be damage (74%), not checking the
expiration date (61%), and not discussing condom use with a partner before sex (60%). In addition, various technical errors were
found, including putting on the condom after starting sex (43%),
taking off the condom before sex was over (15%), not leaving a
space at the tip of the condom (40%), and placing the condom
upside down on the penis and then having to flip it over (30%).
29% of study participants reported condom breakage and 13%
reported that the condom slipped off during sex.

Still, most people at some point do have unprotected
sex, so make sure you take all the steps necessary to prevent
an unwanted pregnancy and to diagnose and treat an STD.

Linda Says:
*A pivotal time in high school was soon after I got my
license and a good friend asked if I'd be willing to drive
her to Portland so she could get an abortion. Being the
helper/nurturer that I am, I didn't have any qualms
about helping her and didn't take much time to worry*

about what I believed or didn't believe. But I lied to my parents that she and I, as well as a guy friend of ours, were going shopping. On the 60 mile trip, she threw up several times. We waited with her at the Lovejoy Surgery Center. But once she went in, we had a few hours to kill. I remember walking around downtown Portland not really putting it all together what she was going through. She cried and held her belly all the way home.

A few days later, I was having horrible cramps while taking a hot bath and my mom came in to check on me. I cried to her that I had lied to them and I felt awful about it. I ended up telling her about the whole affair. My progressive mom handled the news very well. My friend pulled away from me after that like I was too big a reminder of it all. We didn't really connect much again. Later, at our graduation, I received flowers from her parents. She had told them recently about the whole thing and they wanted to thank me for taking care of her. I know that those decisions made by my boyfriend and I to fool around but not to have sex were partly because I didn't want to get pregnant, have that decision to make, and possibly screw up my chances of being a teacher.

Coping with Groping

When you're behind the wheel of a car, jamming down the accelerator and going from zero-to-sixty as fast as possible isn't good for the car or for the driver, though that is how many young men drive. That is also how many young men approach sex. They're horny, they want sex, you're right there so full speed ahead. If you feel the same, then go for it. But if not? It helps to be very clear what your personal standards are and then stick to them because you will be the rare woman if you're never pressured to have sex.

Men who expect women to "put out" are sexist, ego-centric and feel entitled to get what they want regardless of how the other person feels. Empathy and mutuality are not values they embrace. Consequently, if you find yourself entangled with one of these Neanderthals, it'll be up to you to act decisively to remove yourself when things have gone far enough for you. For guys like this, "no" doesn't mean "no". It means "try harder".

So if and when you've had enough, don't feel like you need to get his permission to stop. Just say no. Stand up. Put on any clothes that were removed. Leave the room. Don't worry about "making him mad" or leaving him sexually frustrated. Nobody ever died from unreleased sexual tension.

Linda Says:
Once when I was in college, during my second year, I had finally succumbed to the idea that parties were the place to meet guys. My roommate and I both had no problem telling guys we weren't going to have sex with them. Some of those guys would still want to "walk us home" and we would let them and even invite them in to make out. I think that in their alcohol-induced states, they would think they could get more out of us. I think we were really lucky neither of us had a date rape situation as these guys were pretty much strangers to us. Some left mad but no one tried to hurt us.

46

CHAPTER FIVE

DATING AND VIOLENCE

❧

This Day and Age

This is not a fun chapter to write and probably won't be a fun chapter to read. I am so sad that in preparing you for adulthood I still have to talk about ways to protect yourself from dating violence. Most of the women I interviewed for this book all had cautionary tales they wanted to impart. The truth is that all women are potential rape victims, dependent upon the decency of men and our own ability to protect ourselves.

It's not comfortable to think this way, like you're a walking potential rape victim. Many women choose denial over awareness. I don't want you to do that. I want you to be aware of the risks so you can take sensible precautions, just like wearing a seatbelt when you drive. Car accidents are the leading cause of death of young people yet everyone travels by car. Just because car accidents can and do happen to some people doesn't mean you will be in a car accident. Same with dating violence. In this day and age, it's better to be prepared with all the tools at your disposal so, if at all possible, your life won't be derailed by violence and instead you can enjoy the healthy expression of your sexuality in a trusting relationship.

College and Sexual Violence

While females of every age are always vulnerable to sexual violence, young women going off to college are vulnerable in new ways due to the college lifestyle.

First of all, parties, with illegal drug use and underage drinking are prevalent, especially at schools with fraternities, sororities and big athletic programs. It doesn't matter if drinking, drugs, and sexual harassment are against school, dormitory, Greek, or athletic policy. Determined students always find a way to party. As everyone knows from all the D.A.R.E. and Health Ed classes, drinking and drugs lower inhibitions and inhibit rational thinking. Young women under the influence are less able to spot potential danger and to act when they do, and young men under the influence can get aggressive, especially when in groups.

Another aspect of college is that attending the same school gives the illusion everyone is a friend. Colleges actively promote solidarity through social programming which can ease homesickness, improve morale, and provide social support for stressed out students. You will make friends in college, good friends, perhaps life-long friends. However, the plain fact of college life is that thousands of total strangers are thrown together night and day in close quarters. These strangers will not all be safe. Part of your job at this age is to figure out who is trustworthy and who is not.

Linda Says:
There was a party where I had to go into a back room
to grab a coat and had to get through a big group of

baseball players. One of them grabbed my butt as I tried to make it through them. As I turned to ask him to stop, several others began grabbing me and I was kind of spinning in the midst of this circle with them grabbing at me. They were laughing and I was panicking. I finally bolted out and asked a big guy who was a good friend to retrieve my coat. He hit at least one of the guys if not more and I cannot remember if I ever got my coat. That was the closest I'd ever come to a forced situation and it was so uncomfortable. I remember feeling panicky in certain crowds after that for some time.

Date Rape

Rape, sodomy, sexual assault: Ugly words for ugly acts that all have a legal, statutory definition. I encourage you to look up their definitions. For the purposes of this book, I'll just say that you have the right to choose when, where, how, and

> 2.8% of college women experience rape, either completed or attempted.
>
> In 9 out of 10 of these cases, the rapist was someone the victim knew, such as a boyfriend, friend, or acquaintance.
>
> 22.8% of college rape-victims are multiple-rape victims.

with whom you are sexual. If you have not chosen or are unable to choose because you are incapacitated, then any forced sexual contact will meet some legal definition of sexual assault. Basically, if saying no is not an option—whether due to force, threats, coercion or incapacitation—then you have been the victim of assault.

Many campuses have education campaigns about sexual assault, including what is termed "date rape". Date rape, or

CAITLIN CLAIRE DIEHL

"acquaintance rape" refers to the fact that the perpetrator of the assault is known to the victim. This type of assault is far more common than the knife-wielding stranger jumping out of the bushes, though that happens, too. It happened exactly that way to a friend of mine when she was a college student. Far more typical is what happened to me:

Caitlin's Story:

I was a freshman in college, excited and eager for all that life would hold. In the fall of my first year I was invited to the birthday party of an upper classman, in fact, a Resident Advisor in a neighboring dorm. I didn't particularly like the guy but I was super flattered and was reassured that my brother and his girlfriend, who was one of my best friends, would be there.

Turns out the "party" was just the four of us in the birthday boy's dorm room with plenty of beer and snacks. I'd never had any alcohol before, had never received any education about drinking other than being told I shouldn't drink, so had no idea about how to drink responsibly. So I drank beer like water and in a very short period of time became incapacitated. So did my brother and his girlfriend who fell asleep on the dorm room floor.

Details after that are fuzzy but I know the guy picked me up and put me on his bed, a top bunk. He took off my clothes and put my head down to his penis and put it in my mouth. I was repulsed and wanted to get away but I couldn't get my body to act or my mouth to speak. I was so drunk it was like I was trapped in my body, which didn't work anymore. Some time later, when he was done and got off of me, I got up, got dressed and stumbled back to my dorm room and tried to forget that night ever happened.

The next year I heard from a friend of mine that the guy did the exact same thing to several other freshman girls in her dorm, getting them liquored up and then assaulting them. That's when I realized I'd been set-up and raped. Before that, I blamed myself for getting drunk and not "handling" the situation. I was seriously emotionally messed up for years but I never got any help until I developed PTSD around the 10-year anniversary of the assault. Then I got the help I needed and was able to heal.

Control Freaks Make Bad Boyfriends

On the Internet you can easily locate the warning signs that identify a guy who is a potential abuser. Here are a few problematic behaviors:

- Jealousy
- Controlling behavior
- Quick involvement
- Unrealistic expectations
- Isolation
- Blames others for problems
- Blames others for their feelings
- Hypersensitivity
- Rigid sex roles
- Extreme mood swings

Some women can perceive possessiveness, jealousy or other controlling behaviors as a proof of love. Really, they are proof of insecurity and a lack of respect for your autonomy. Another trap women can fall into is being willing to take the blame for your man's moods or behaviors so as not to rock the boat. If you find yourself regularly holding back what you really think or not doing what you really want so as "not to make him mad," you have a problem.

The following behaviors are much more obviously dangerous as they involve more overt violence or threat of violence. Still, if you grew up in a home where violence was normal, you may not even realize the danger you are in. Run the other way as quickly as you can if the guy you like demonstrates any of these behaviors:

- ♦ Cruelty to animals or children
- ♦ "Playful" use of force during sex
- ♦ History of abusing others in previous relationships
- ♦ Threats of violence or abuse
- ♦ Breaking objects
- ♦ Use of force during an argument

I urge you to look up further details and explanations of the above behaviors (http://www.northwestern.edu/ womenscenter/issues-information/relationship-violence/ warning-signs-abusive-person.html). It's important and may save you a world of trouble. However, in the interests of saving you valuable time, I know a fool-proof method for identifying guys who are lousy boyfriend material. You ready? Here it is: Just avoid the assholes.

Good Sex After Abuse

Victims of violence often have invisible wounds that must be healed in order to have a healthy sense of their own sexuality. Sexual violence can destroy a woman's sense of security. As a way to reestablish that security, we might adopt one of two attitudes about sex: either we become very controlling, needing things to be just so, or we grow to be indiscriminate as a way of proving that we are just fine and are in control of our bodies and our sexuality. Neither are good foundations for the genuine expression of a healthy sexuality. A good sexual relationship starts with trust and that has been destroyed when someone has been abused or raped.

Reestablishing basic trust is necessary in order to heal. To assist with that healing, I'm a big proponent of therapy, though it took me years to realize I needed it myself. Being in a relationship with a kind and caring person can help as well. The important first step is to recognize that you've been wounded and to know that healing is possible.

Partnering Someone Who Has Been Abused

Whether you're paired up with a man or a woman, you might discover that your partner was abused or assaulted at some point in his or her life. Patience will be your friend as you both work through how this past abuse might be affecting your relationship. You will discover, often by accident, what your partner's triggers are, the things that set him/her off and make intimacy difficult. Educating yourself about the effects of abuse will help you to not take your partner's reactivity personally. Talking with each other and with a therapist can help both of you navigate any difficulties either of

> Child sexual abuse is believed to affect 10-25% of girls worldwide. In studies conducted mostly in developed countries, 5–10% of men report being sexually abused as children.

you are having with being close. All of the virtues of any good relationship—compassion, kindness, trust, affection, humor—are especially important when coping with the long-term effects of violence.

Of course, this presumes that you care enough about the person and the relationship to put in that kind of emotional work. You don't have to. You can opt to back away because you're not ready to tackle anything that heavy with this particular person.

Protecting yourself from sexual violence starts with awareness of your surroundings, good instincts about people, and trust in your own radar about what is safe and what isn't.

Safety Precautions:

- *Don't be an ostrich*: Educate yourself about dating violence, sexual assault and sexual harassment.
- *Stay aware:* Be aware of your surroundings, who you're with, and any warning signs of danger.
- *Trust yourself*: If someone or something doesn't feel right, get away.
- *Have an exit strategy*: Know your location and how to safely get home from there; carry money and a cell phone.
- *Protect yourself*: Take a self-defense class. Put your personal safety above social niceties. Nice girls do get mad.
- *Seek help*: If something does happen, report it to the police, a rape crisis center or the campus health center.

I hope that educating yourself about the worst that can happen will propel you to adopt habitual safety precautions that allow you to enjoy the best that relationships can offer.

Chapter Six

Commitment and Sex

∞

I'd like to make the sweeping statement that commitment between partners leads to the best sex but I can't because it isn't true for everybody. What I can say is that commitment fosters trust. Trust makes it easier for people to relax, let go and feel deeply, which allows intimacy to develop. This, in turn, allows a sexual relationship to transcend the mere physical and opens the door to a profound emotional and, dare I say, spiritual connection that enriches one's life like nothing else can.

If you're into that kind of thing.

Sarah Says:
There have been times I've tried satisfying my physical and sexual hunger by making out with a guy but I nearly always regret it for there is no emotional intimacy between us to give the experience any meaning or to be truly gratifying. It's an empty pleasure, like sucking on a sugar candy when what I really want is steak and potatoes. Only touch with love is food for our souls. Part of me wishes I could be out having sex without

commitment, soaking in that intimacy, having someone's arms wrapped around my naked body, losing control. But my deeper wisdom knows that as beautiful and natural as that desire is, physical intimacy without soul intimacy first would leave me with a hurt far deeper and more lasting than any orgasm would give me pleasure.

Mr. Right vs. Mr. Right Now

What kind of commitment do you need before you're ready to get naked with somebody? Do you need to be married or at least engaged? What about if you're in an exclusive, couple relationship? Do you want to know somebody for a while first or are you okay acting on instant attraction?

Your answers to these questions will take some thought and possibly some experimentation. You might find the answer varies depending on circumstances as well as the man in question. We've all seen the movie where the commitment-phobic boyfriend breaks up with the heroine because she wants to get married and have kids only to see him immediately get married and have kids with another woman, further breaking the heroine's heart, (until she finds her real Mr. Right who was waiting under her nose the whole time!).

When personal standards war with sexual chemistry, standards often lose the battle, especially when you're young and still figuring things out. If that's the case, be kind to yourself and try to hold to your line next time.

On the other hand, you may discover you are quite happy to connect sexually whenever there's a spark. You're all right hanging with Mr. Right Now without needing any pledges of commitment or long-lasting love. In this case, you value the connection in the moment and don't want anything more than that.

You'll have to learn for yourself what works best for you, letting your experiences and your values shape the choices you make.

MaryKate Says:
Most of my friends are married and divorced already. I'm sure you won't want to hear this but HONESTLY *the ones who are still together waited to have sex until they were married and they are still madly in love with one another. I'm sure you're thinking I'm old fashioned, but from what I've seen on the "type A" East Coast, having sex too early just harms the girls. Maybe on the West Coast people are built differently, but here—with all the pressure of academics, jobs, making it—it's just one more unnecessary burden for college girls.*

Welcome to Neverland

Men in their thirties and forties who have perfected commitment-avoidance are called "Peter Pans". I'm not sure what the female equivalent is called. Still, there are adults out there who have made avoiding commitment an art form. These types are often fun to be with, socially adept, sexually experienced, and full of romantic gestures. And that's as far as things go. After a while, you realize there is no increased sharing of personal information or feelings, no meeting their friends or family. Your time with them is all surface and no depth, all gloss and no substance.

People like this avoid commitment as a way of avoiding complications—like other people's feelings, needs, or expectations. Peter Pans don't like messes; no matter how old they are, they act like perpetual adolescents who refuse to grow up. "Let's just keep things light," is a common catchphrase of Peter Pans. Of course, the minute two people connect sexually, you're hip deep in complications. But by not committing, the Peter Pans of the world can pretend those messy aspects of hooking up don't exist. Basically, by not committing to your sex partner once you're out of bed, you're saying that you are unwilling to acknowledge or work through any of those complications that ALWAYS arise.

This sounds like bad news for relationships and in 30-40 year olds, it is a red flag. However, this is EXACTLY how 18-24 year-olds are hard-wired to behave. Young adulthood is a kind of Neverland where adult roles and behaviors are tried on to see which ones fit best. Most people your age are learning the skills you need to make it on your own. Your life and your path are all about you and what you want. Other people's needs and considerations often come a distant second, especially if your job or school or family is very demanding.

Of course, people mature at different rates and it is a well-documented and much-bemoaned fact that women mature faster than men. After all, that frontal lobe—responsible for thinking about consequences before acting and being aware of the effect of one's behavior on other people—doesn't fully develop until the mid twenties. Consequently, depending on developmental factors, you may find a mismatch between the level of commitment you want out of a relationship versus what your guy wants. Or the other way around. The key is to be aware that you are now living in Neverland where Peter Pans of both sexes happily play their days away.

So welcome to the island where your main task is to learn to fly on your own. In order to do that, believe in yourself, sprinkle your own pixie dust and create your own magic. Test your wings. Try new things. Even enjoy Peter Pan (or being a Peter Pan) if you want. Just be aware of his limitations and don't expect more than he (or you) is able to give at this phase of your lives.

Committed Relationships

Say you're one of those who mature early and you're thinking about wanting a committed relationship. This ups the emotional stakes quite a bit and it's worth thinking about what a commitment might mean. Commitment implies an investment, at least for a time, in the other person and in your relationship and a willingness to communicate and compromise about your individual needs in order to make the relationship work.

That is, until one or both of you is no longer willing to communicate or to compromise. Then you break up, which can be messy and painful, a natural growing apart with no hard feelings, or something in between.

A committed relationship progresses through a series of choices made by each person each of which can do one of three things:

- ♦ Split you up
- ♦ Maintain the status quo
- ♦ Deepen your connection

When you're young, those choices circle around the following areas:

- ♦ *Fidelity*: A committed relationship means the two of you are exclusive, you're not dating or sleeping

61

with anyone else, that you're "a couple", boyfriend and girlfriend. Cheating on your boyfriend or girlfriend is a betrayal of trust and that commitment. It's also incredibly common, especially when one is a young adult. (Remember that still-developing frontal lobe!).

♦ *Flirting*. Does being exclusive also mean neither of you flirts with the guy or gal sitting next to you in class or at work? Or notices that hottie passing you on the street? Or does it just mean that while you may experience other attractions, you don't act on that attraction? People have different acceptance levels for flirting so be sure and discuss it.

♦ *Time*. Do you expect to see each other every day? Whenever both of you has free time? Sleep over every night? Call or text regularly? Go out on a date every Friday and/or Saturday? What kind of breathing room do you each need in the relationship?

♦ *Priorities*. This is, I think, one of the trickiest aspects of commitment to navigate, especially when you're first making your way in life. Presumably, the two of you are in school and/or working. You have individual friends, personal goals, career aspirations, and job opportunities. How well do your own plans mesh with your boyfriend's? Is the relationship worth you sacrificing or postponing your personal dreams? Is being together so important that you're willing to let your boyfriend give up his goals?

Walking Down the Aisle

Some people's main goal in life is to get married and have a family. Some religions and cultures point to this as the preferred (or only) dream that a woman should have. Being married myself with a daughter I adore, I fully support wanting to be a wife and mother when you're ready, when it is your own choice, your own dream. However, when young women settle down before they've had a chance to really live any other dreams apart from getting married and having a family because that's what someone else said they should do or because they're afraid of being on their own, then that marriage and those children can become a trap.

When a couple is in love, wanting to be together forever is the natural culmination of that love. My personal recommendation for women is that before getting married, a woman should have the skills and experience necessary to be self-supporting and should have spent some time doing just that.

Intimacy

Commitment deepens intimacy. This is a sweeping statement I CAN make. Intimacy with another person is the sublime experience of love, closeness, connection and belonging, of togetherness. This is one of the deepest human needs and can be experienced in many different kinds of emotional relationships: between siblings, parents and children, and best friends. However, the intimacy experienced by a committed couple who have an emotional AND sexual relationship is in a category all its own.

A couple's level of intimacy—in bed and out—develops over time. As partners develop trust in one another, they feel safe enough to reveal their deepest needs and fears. When those revelations are met with support, then intimacy is enhanced. Communication is at the heart of intimacy, communication through words and actions.

Interestingly, some people find it easier to bare their bodies than bare their souls. If you're one of these types, you might be comfortable having sex without any kind of connection beyond the physical. If not, that's important to know about yourself as well. Also, know that your intimacy needs can change over time as you grow and mature and as your boyfriend grows and matures (or doesn't).

Sexual Appetites: Desert or Dessert

Here's an old joke: A woman is dishing with her girlfriends saying, "He wants to have sex ALL the time, like twice a week! I wish he would just get off me!" The boyfriend is having a beer with his buddies, confiding, "We NEVER have sex, like only twice a week. It's killing me!"

Whether your sex life with your partner is a sexual feast or famine depends all on your point of view. It can also depend on one's expectations for how you think you're supposed to feel about sex and what your expectations of men are.

While there is cultural pressure on women to *look* sexy, the pressure on men is to *act* sexually, to be ever-ready to hop into bed with a woman. Our media saturates us with images that unconsciously influence how we expect others to behave, especially in areas of romantic and sexual behavior. Believe it or not, neither men nor women are always in the mood for sex.

Science also tells us the peak of male sexuality is late teens to early twenties while women don't peak until our forties. Right there, biology sets us up for a comedy of errors.

So, if your guy doesn't want to have sex with you, it doesn't necessarily mean he no longer loves you or finds you attractive. If you find that your desire for sex runs at a different speed than your guy's, know there is nothing wrong with either of you. As with any other differences between two people, you're going to have to talk about what you need and want, ask what your partner needs and wants, and try to reach some sort of resolution that both people agree to. Not very sexy is it?

> *Rachel Says:*
> *I think that it's God's existential joke that he made men and women attracted to each other so they got the idea that they were supposed to be with each other, you know. And they're entirely different species.*

Sexual Practices

I said in the beginning this was not a sex manual and I still mean that. I just want to mention what behaviors give sexual pleasure to people are as diverse and varied as people themselves. Don't be too hasty in judging a partner's turn-ons, or your own, as perverted. When you've got a committed and willing partner, it can be quite fun to explore and discover the variety of what you both find pleasurable.

Information about sex abounds. There are Internet

> While vaginal intercourse is still the most common sexual behavior reported by adults, many sexual events do not involve intercourse and include only partnered masturbation or oral sex.

65

sites, books, videos, and bricks-and-mortar storefronts dedicated to sexual pleasure and it's not all pornography. There are plenty of materials and educational or relationship-enhancing information available. Be aware that while some sex shops are sleazy, and some just cater to gay men, there are others catering to women and straight couples. Even without a partner, you can still educate yourself about the world of sex.

> There is enormous variability in the sexual repertoires of U.S. adults, with more than 40 combinations of sexual activity described at adults' most recent sexual event.

At the same time, just because your partner finds something to be a turn-on, doesn't mean you have to go along with it and vice versa. I can't stress that enough. If your relationship is going to thrive, then both parties need to be willing and open to any proposed sexual activity before trying it out. If not, then saying no to it must be an accepted and supported part of your relationship.

On the other hand, I'd also like to mention that even if the sexual behavior between the two (or more) of you is consensual, that doesn't necessarily make it healthy in the long run. As an extreme example, two people may smoke crack before having sex because of the rush, but that doesn't make it good for them. Check in with yourself after a sexual encounter and you will know whether or not that experience was in your best interest.

Pornography

Back in my young-adult years, mainstream heterosexual pornography came in the form of magazines like *Playboy*,

Penthouse and *Hustler*. While sex chat lines and porn films existed, access wasn't as easy as it is now. The Internet has opened the floodgates to all sorts of media, including pornography. As pornography has become more accessible, pornography use and abuse has soared, especially among men.

> Over half of all spending on the Internet is estimated to be related to sex. US porn revenues have been estimated to exceed the combined revenues of companies like ABC, CBS, and NBC.

Not all sexually explicit materials are pornographic. Some fall under the heading of art or education. Some couples incorporate sexually explicit media into their love-making and find it enhances their relationship. Whether or not certain materials are pornographic, I leave it up to you to decide. As Supreme Court Justice Potter Stewart famously said about pornography, "I know it when I see it."

Pornography is a problem in a relationship if your partner's using it bothers you. It's also a problem if your guy prefers pornography to having sex with you. Pornography portrays sexual fantasies of a certain kind, not real life. If

> In a national study, 14% of people reported having used a sexually explicit website. In the same study, 25% of men reported visiting a pornographic site in the previous 30 days; 4% of women reported visiting pornographic sites in the same timeframe.

your guy wants you to behave more like his favorite porn star, he's not appreciating the real woman in front of him and you had best give him the boot.

Your man should find you sexy, just as you are, and not ask you to change your look to conform to some image put in his head by the porn industry. If you prefer wearing sweatshirts and jeans and the idea of thigh-high boots just irritates you, don't let some guy's porn-fueled image of what's sexy in a woman influence you. I still remember seeing a movie that portrayed in all seriousness the lead actress vacuuming naked except for high heels. I never laughed so hard. Talk about fantasy!

Sexual Fantasies

The imagination is a wonderful gift and has a huge role in the sex life of human beings. Visualization techniques using our imaginations support success in endeavors from business to athletics. Picturing something in our minds enables us to try out an experience without ever enacting it in real life. Sexual fantasies provide an outlet for sexual feelings and activities that we might not have the opportunity or desire to act out in real life.

I'm going to repeat that: Many sexual fantasies represent feelings that people do not want to act out in real life. Just because you imagine something and find the imagining pleasurable does not mean you would find acting it out equally so. Sexual fantasies occur in the privacy of our minds. It is a very personal decision whether or not to share or enact those fantasies with another person.

> Men's sexual fantasies tend to be more sexually explicit than women's; women's fantasies tend to be more emotional and romantic.

Sexual Skill

Not everybody is good in bed. There, I've said it. As one friend said to me when we were in high school, "Boys are just so frantic!" Young men's motors rev pretty quickly under many circumstances while women's sexual response tends to be more finely tuned. Young, inexperienced men may lack finesse which women may find off-putting, even when they like the guy. Young women may have no idea how men are calibrated and will be unsure what to do with all that unfamiliar equipment. This lack of experience or expertise can be quite disappointing on both sides if you're expecting to get your mind blown during sex.

Other shortcomings you might run across include a lack of technique, ambivalence towards the person or about being sexually active, unfamiliarity with anatomy, and insensitivity to your emotional needs. The good news is that pleasuring someone is learned behavior that definitely can improve with practice.

If your sex partner is a short-term hookup, then investing the time, energy and communication necessary to maximize your sexual experience just may not be worth it. If you and your sex partner are invested in one another, then definitely spend mattress time figuring out what each other enjoys. This should be homework you enjoy!

Sexual Relationships Over Time

When a couple first fall in love, sex is usually a big part of their relationship. Over time, this urgency naturally eases up. Over how much time and how much does it ease up? This is impossible to predict. Just be aware that people change. Relationships change. Sex lives change. That's life and something we all have to learn to cope with.

Whether you're partnered or not, the external pressures of work, school and family can wreak havoc on one's sex drive. Illness, anger, grief, moving, job loss, closeted sexual preferences, poor school or work performance—all these can affect interest in sex. Getting older certainly does, as does having children.

So, if your sex life has changed and you're not happy about it, I'll bet you know by now what advice I'm going to give: Talk about it! Whether the issue is changes in your sex life or whose turn it is to do the dishes, successfully navigating the stressors in any relationship means talking over your needs and those of your partner.

CHAPTER SEVEN

LIGHTS ON THE PATH

☙

So, that's it. That's all I know. Well, not everything. I could write another whole book just on marriage and sex but that's for another time. I hope you found the book helpful, that you learned something, and maybe laughed a time or two. I hope you feel clearer about your own sexual values, limits, hopes and expectations—for yourself and for the boys/men you date.

I just want to leave you with one last thought. Some have characterized a woman's life as having three phases: Maiden, Mother and Crone. The Maiden phase is girlhood and young adulthood. Motherhood, whether children ever come, is a woman's middle life where she commits to a life path and/or partner and expends her fertility (i.e. her creative powers) at work and/or at home. Menopause initiates women into the Crone phase of life where latent interests and talents can flower and one's accumulated life experience and wisdom can be passed on to the next generation.

Each phase is special, each phase has its own gifts and challenges, but I want to lobby hard in this book for the joys of the Maiden. Whether or not you choose to be sexually

active, the gifts of the Maiden are about the joys of self-dis-
covery, learning about who you are through varied life experiences, and finding and taking your place in the world.
The Maiden is all about becoming. This is a process, often
a stressful one for young people who are eager to figure out
their post-high school life path and cruise down it as quickly
as possible on the way to fulfilling their dreams.

I urge you not to be in such a hurry. Take your time
with commencing sexual activity, with choosing a career,
and with declaring what you're going to be when you grow
up. New adulthood (ages 18-24) is an in-between time.
You're not a child but you're not an adult either, though at
times life requires you to take on an adult's responsibilities
and burdens. The uncertainty of not knowing how your life
is going to turn out can feel quite scary and it can lead to
premature decisions to settle down, pick a college major or
a career path, just to have something decided, something
certain, something to hang on to.

Resist this impulse. Embrace the uncertainty, try new
things, meet lots of people, take a variety of classes, explore
different jobs. Don't just keep your nose to the grindstone,
your eye on the prize. Remember to look up, notice the
color of the sky, the temperature of the air. Take a walk.
Breathe deeply. Feel how alive you are. You. Your unique,
one and only life. Embrace it!

APPENDIX

THE LIGHT FROM THREE LAMPS

◌

Within the chapters you just read are snippets of stories from various women, just a fraction of the stories and life lessons shared with me for this book. In this appendix I've included three longer stories from three women who are traveling paths far different from one another. I wanted to highlight just how uniquely personal our choices are around sex and relationships, and how we each must find our own way.

All the women in this book hope that the light from their lives will shine like a lamp upon your own path, making your travels that much easier.

◌

Lamplight One: Parker Lee

My sex talk consisted of my mother giving a me a large picture book with drawn characters and pretty much all I remember learning was masturbation is BAD! NOT good. NOT necessary. A big fat NO-NO. So okay, I hear ya. I had not done anything like that yet so okay, one more thing for a good Christian girl to steer clear of. So noted.

Fast forward four years - At 19 I get married to my first real boyfriend.. I don't know how to ask for what I need or want. Even if I know how to ask, I don't know what to ask for. I am unsure and uneducated. I only know what he has taught me, which looking back, wasn't a whole lot (bless his 20 year old heart). I'm not satisfied in our sex life—I had romanticized so much more than this—and neither is he, evidenced by the string of girlfriends he has during our marriage.

Fast forward five and a half years and I am going through a divorce—I am now the mother of a two year old and three month old. Note: no masturbation has taken place at this point. A few months pass and I meet a guy. We date. We have sex—at 25 I have now had two sexual partners. Although these men share the same name, they are nothing alike in bed. My eyes are beginning to open. Interesting. My boyfriend gets a job out of state. He moves away and I am left sexually hungry. Still no masturbation—the cartoon character said it was wrong and not necessary—Christians don't do this. To be honest, it just never occurred to me. Months pass and my body is calling out to me for attention growing louder and louder. She is hard to ignore any longer. I begin exploring. Shame. But I also feel good and am curious.

I meet a new man. We marry. We have a child together and he adopts my two older children. I am now 27 and have three daughters. He's my third sexual partner. There's anger and an abusive side to him that begins to put a distance between my heart and him. I don't want to have sex with him, but do because it's easier than dealing with his wrath. He's okay in bed—very determined. If I don't have an orgasm, he's hurt and angry and tries more and longer and harder. I become a damn fine actress during my marriage to him. I begin to wonder if I'm gay. I don't want sex; I am repulsed. I feel a hunger deep inside but I withhold that part of me from him.

A man six years my junior begins showing an interest in me. When he steals a kiss from me, I realize that I am not gay, but I simply don't like or trust my husband. We have sex two times. It's all about him. Okay. I'm beginning to see a pattern here.

Eleven years pass. I am a single mom again with a grade schooler, a middle schooler, and a high schooler. I am determined to be on my own. I don't need or want a man. My body calls to me. I answer her! I begin to get to know this body of mine. What feels good. How much pressure. Timing. Oh! What's this new sensation? At the age of 36, I am truly, for the first time, getting to know my body. I know what I want. I know what I like. I know what I don't like. And then it hits me—how can someone else figure out what I need and want if I don't even know? I feel empowered. I feel knowledgeable. I feel in control of my own body. I feel like instead of sex happening to me, that I can fully participate and take part in someone making love to me.

So at 39 I get married again. This husband, my third and FINAL, gets a very different wife than husband number one and number two. I am confident. I am fully engaged and most of the time, the driving force of our sex life. Things are good for three years then something changes in our sex life. I am now ready to be pursued by him. I want to feel sought after, to have a fully engaged sexual partner—I am now in my 40s after all! His 20 year marriage contained very little sex so having a wife who initiated sex was healing for him. He gets lazy and his body begins to change. My husband is 15 years older than me and I am left unattended as he silently struggles with his body and his physical reaction to me changing. Without much notice, I don't realize what is happening and neither does my husband.

I am wooed by another man six years older than me. To have a fully engaged sexual partner eager to learn and explore is healing for me—he is the driving force and I feel desired. I have learned much about my body and how to be fully engaged in sex now. My heart quickly gets involved with this man. I have to break it off after a few months. I love my husband—he is so good to me and my daughters love their stepdad. I end the relationship with this other man.

Feeling quite lost and obviously sending out those signals loud and clear unbeknownst to me at the time, a man 15 years my junior kisses me one night at a bar. I am there celebrating a friend's birthday. He is an incredible kisser. When he and I kiss, it is an art. I kid you not, it is something to behold. He is hungry. I am hungry. I love having sex with him. He knows what he is doing. He is young and has lots of energy. Finally! Someone who can keep up with me! Orgasms are plentiful. Four...five...six in a row. I am in heaven. He reads my body language and listens to my audible signs. He knows what I want and need, sometimes even before I know. I have never felt so sexually alive. Neither of us are passive or shy. We are both fully engaged and eager to please one another and feel pleasure. This relationship is where my love of being on top comes from. A woman having ultimate control over her orgasm is something that can't be taught, I don't think. If you stumble upon it and happen to realize the treasure you've found, then your sex life is forever changed and for the better. Six orgasms, people!!! That has to be a record!

I end this on-again-off-again relationship after nine months. I decide that even though I am having the time of my life sexually that I am becoming someone I can't respect. I want me back. I was a good girl growing up and in my early years and I think there's nothing wrong with being a good girl, there are less devastating consequences to deal with, but I learn many important sexual lessons late in life. To be awakened to your own sexuality by exploring it is empowering and means you have a better chance at 'teaching' that special someone how to make love to you. If you don't know what you like or want, then you are a moving target (women kind of are anyway), and you are probably setting someone up for failure because you can't obtain something that is obscure.

Moral of the story—Masturbation is our friend! My mom was wrong, the book was wrong—it is truly a gift to yourself and your future sexual partner(s) to explore who you are and what makes you sexually tick.

LampLight Two: Sarah

As a single adult, I am rarely touched in any kind of intimate, affectionate way beyond the casual hug. It's painful not to be lovingly touched and my heart aches for human closeness. Once, years ago, when an older friend cupped my face in her hands then hugged me, she didn't just hug, but held me tightly to her with a fierce love. When I'm lonely and need to feel someone close by, I soak in these memories, letting them wash over me—remembering the few times I have felt someone's love through my skin, felt wrapped in their deep affection. Sometimes I cry for such physical tenderness whether from a friend or a lover—a basic human need rarely gratified in my life. In our culture, intimate touch between friends is just not done and I desperately miss it.

There have been times I've tried satisfying my physical and sexual hunger by making out with a guy but I nearly always regret it for there is no emotional intimacy between us to give the experience any meaning or to be truly gratifying. It's an empty pleasure, like sucking on a sugar candy when what I really want is steak and potatoes. Only touch with love is food for our souls. Part of me wishes I could be out having sex without commitment, soaking in that intimacy, having someone's arms wrapped around my naked body, losing control. But my deeper wisdom knows that as beautiful and natural as that desire is, physical intimacy without soul intimacy first would leave me with a hurt far deeper and more lasting than any orgasm would give me pleasure. To trust someone that deeply with my body, I want us to have already trusted each other with what's in our hearts. I know the only way I'm going to get what I want is by truly loving the person first. This truth has made me cautious in who I let touch me and who I touch. If I'm not close to someone emotionally, I don't want to be touched by them. Even when I get a massage, a healthy way to be touched in addition to the bodily benefits, I enjoy it far more if I'm on friendly terms with the person giving it. If the time comes I do decide to make a life-long commitment to another person, then we will be making love and not merely sliding our bodies against each other.

Finding a man is not on my priority list, though. I believe joining my life to another ought to be a blessing for both of us, a gift on top of an already fulfilling existence full of fun, interesting projects, and love, not to complete it. If I meet someone along that road and we love each other, then I will have another great joy in my life. Living a life of abstinence has its *own* gifts, things I've come to value. I have so much fun pursuing my passions, working on projects, and traveling without taking anyone else into account. With all that time and energy normally spent on a relationship, I can invest instead in the world and the people around me— giving my love out and going on adventures. My unfulfilled need for physical closeness and intimacy has also drawn me into God's arms innumerable times. Being more aware of God's presence and feeling his/her closeness has given me abiding strength, deep comfort, and lasting joy for this is *true* intimacy and our time together has become my center, my ballast, my life. When I do need to express my sexuality in a physical way, I make love to myself and though I know it's not the same as being touched by another, it still brings a physical release. By living an abstinent life, I'm not ignoring my sexuality, simply expressing it in a different way.

Lamplight Three: Rachel

I was never with somebody I wanted to marry. I was in two very long-term relationships where the other person wanted us to get married. I loved both people very much and I loved our relationship, but I was really clear I didn't want to be married to them and marry my life to their life.

Over the years I felt like I did the opposite of what most people seemed to do because most people seemed to say, "Here are this person's great qualities and so I want to marry them." While both of these people had wonderful qualities, excellent qualities, those good qualities were not the parts that I wanted to avoid. I had friends say to me, "He's a great guy," and, "He's this, this and this," and I would say, "That isn't the part I don't want to live with." Somehow, it's funny because I'm very much an optimistic, half-full kind of person, but I felt like I didn't want to bind myself with the parts of them that I didn't want to live with. It was their shortcomings that got in the way of my binding my life to theirs.

I was 21 when I first met "Rob". We were together for 12 years. We had opposite experiences growing up that I think contributed to our worldview. He came from a struggling background—his mother died when he was five—and so he was, on the one hand, a very upbeat person who was very funny. He made me laugh all the time. But he had this sort of cynical view of life—like you have to work as hard as you possibly can and it won't work out anyway—and I had the attitude that you can have or do whatever you want; you just have to go and do what it takes to make that happen. I just knew that he and I had very different worldviews, so even though I was very young at the time, I just felt he would wear down my spirit. I feel like my optimistic disposition is the best gift I've been given in life and I feel some sense of responsibility to honor and protect and nurture that part of me because it does feel like a gift that makes my life good. I just somehow knew on a deep level that to marry Rob would be like a scouring, it would be abrasive to what my spirit is to couple with his spirit.

This was the situation in both of these long-term relationships: while in both cases we shared values deeply, had similar intellects and interests, and could have a really good time with each other, somehow I had this clarity at maybe the soul level or something like that, that I knew I was going to be happier honoring and keeping the strength of my own spirit. That it was going to make me be at peace in life and happy (rather than finding my happiness through pairing up with somebody else).

Once the second relationship ended, I never really thought, "Oh that's it then; now I'll never get married." Every once in a while, I see somebody and I think, "Oh that person seems neat, I could like that person," but I just haven't met somebody that has made me feel like, "Oh, I want to get to know them, I want to be in a relationship with this person." And I meet a lot of people.

I think it's not my frame of mind to think in that way. I've known women through my life, whatever they're doing—they might be checking out a book at the library, they might be buying produce at the grocery store, but whatever else they're doing, they're looking for a man. I mean that is their first agenda and orientation always. And I'm not like that. I don't really know why not but it's not that I haven't thoroughly enjoyed being in a relationship. I have and I really like men but I just haven't met anybody who feels like, "Oh, this person is somebody I'd like to pursue as a partner."

Because I'm single, people share a lot about their relationships with me, mostly their marriages, and you know I haven't really heard about one that made me think, "Oh, I want some of that!" I think that it's God's existential joke that he made men and women attracted to each other so they got the idea that they were supposed to be with each other, you know. And they're entirely different species.

On companionship and loneliness: I have two thoughts about this. I remember as a girl growing up during elementary school, I would walk home from school and hope no one would be there. I have two brothers and my mother was a stay-at-home mom but she did lots of things outside the home and I would just hope that I would have the house to myself, for a little bit of time anyway. So that just gives me a clue that I really liked being alone, but I also have always been very, very social. I loved school because that's where my friends were so it wasn't that I was a loner, but I really liked having time alone. So I think that might be something that is in me that continues. The thought if that I open my calendar and there's nothing on it, that is just fabulous to me. I might enjoy my own company more than most. I might be on the high end of that scale.

I also think that because I didn't have a partner and children, it gave me a lifestyle where friendship has been primary to me. I think it's given me the opportunity to have very deep, as well as wide, friendships. And I continue to have friendships with people I've known since I was two and a half, like my best friend from childhood who was also my neighborhood friend. And I went to my hometown at Thanksgiving and I saw my friend who I went all the way through school with, she and her husband and I are good friends. Also, here where I live, I've been involved in a lot of different things—in my profession I meet a lot of people. So I think that it's given me the opportunity to have very, very satisfying friendships that I could make a priority.

It's really important to me to regularly get together with the people I care about and so I've noticed that not being married has given me the opportunity to have very intimate relationships, with men and women. I've got very close friends, men friends, too. I am a very social person. I like people and so that gives me a lot of satisfaction to have the relationships I have. I think marriage and family uses a lot of one's time and energy and life force. I have more time, energy and life force for a wider range of relationships. So that makes for a very satisfying life for me.

On missing sex: In retrospect, I think the sex kept me in the long-term relationship for a long time, past what it might have been otherwise. The sexual relationship was really good and I think it made the relationship more compelling. I love sex and I've been in really good relationships that way so I don't know how I just go along without this now. I think it's been so long that I'm just used to it.

The other thing I came up with is that dating at my age of 60-something is developmentally inappropriate, that you have to be young and stupid, that you can't, from this vantage point, just casually go out with people. I might be wrong about that but it just seems that you know too much. But I do have this idea that maybe if I met somebody that seemed fun to play with that I might change my mind. It just seems like sex is so compelling that at this stage in life… you know when you're younger, you can just do it, have sex as play and recreation, as something fun. As long as both people know that, that it's the point of why you're having that kind of relationship, just for recreational sex, then that's great. I can't quite see how that would work at this point, though, because it would be so compelling, so connecting. So I can't see having casual sex now. You're not casual in general at this age. Just in general, play, being carefree, is not really part of this time of life. In a way, as all of us get older, we're more carefree because of no children in the home or being retired from work, but emotionally, it's hard to be carefree.

On others' expectations that I marry: My parents know how happy I've been in my life. And I'd have to say I'm one of the happiest people I know. I have a friend who came to visit me and she wrote me a note afterwards saying something like, "This is very clever of you, Rachel, just to have everything just exactly the way you like it." I do think never being married has given me more depth and intimacy and more relationships than a lot of people get to have because of the demands of married life and family life. So it worked for me.

ABOUT THE AUTHOR

ℭ

Caitlin Claire Diehl writes coming-of-age stories for every age. She is the author of the young adult fantasy novel, *First Daughter*, the first in the Web Weaver Chronicles trilogy. Reviews praise, "This book is an excellent read, it was hard to put down!" "Caitlin Claire Diehl writes about the magical process in beautiful prose," and "there are some steamy sex scenes, too!" Look for the second novel in the series, *Second Son*, out in the fall of 2014.

She is also the author of the groundbreaking novel, *In The Name of Love*, the true-to-life, inspiring story of a young woman's recovery from sex abuse and her healing journey towards a life filled with love. Readers call it "sensitive" and "a moving read".

Before turning to writing full time, Caitlin Claire Diehl worked as a counselor and writing instructor. For all the latest, follow Caitlin on Facebook at www.facebook.com/CatilinClaireDiehl or contact her at walncreekpublications@gmail.com. If you like her books, please post reviews on amazon, www.goodreads.com and anywhere else you can think of. Thank you!!!